FIGHTING TO BELONG!

VOL. I: ASIAN AMERICAN, NATIVE HAWAIIAN, AND PACIFIC ISLANDER HISTORY FROM THE 1700s THROUGH THE 1800s

FIGHTING TO BELONG! Asian American, Native Hawaiian, and Pacific Islander History from the 1700s Through the 1800s

A History of Asian Americans, Native Hawaiians, and Pacific Islanders Series Volume I

© 2024 Leading Asian Americans to Unite for Change
Fighting to Belong! Curriculum Guide © 2023–24 The Asian American Education Project

Published by Third State Books and The Asian American Foundation in association with Leading Asian Americans to Unite for Change and The Asian American Education Project.

The Asian American Foundation thanks Amy Chu, her coauthor and son, Alexander Chang, artist Louie Chin, and project manager Pamela Liu for their shared vision and commitment to this groundbreaking endeavor. We are deeply grateful for our partnership with Stewart and Pat Kwoh at The Asian American Education Project and their colleagues, including Virginia Loh-Hagan, Sandy Sakamoto, Samantha Chang, Prabhneek Heer, and Kate Lee. We also acknowledge our friends at Leading Asian Americans to Unite for Change as well as Richard Ting, Terry Park, and Joy Moh at TAAF for their valuable feedback.

Third State Books
93 Cumberland Street
San Francisco, CA 94110
Visit us at www.thirdstatebooks.com

First Third State edition: February 6, 2024

ISBN 979-8-89013-017-4 (trade paperback original)
979-8-89013-019-8 (hardcover)
979-8-89013-018-1 (e-book)

Third State edition designed by AndWorld Design.
Distributed to the book trade worldwide by Publishers Group West.
www.pgw.com / www.ingramcontent.com

Library of Congress Control Number: 2023948169

Printed in Canada by Transcontinental Printing

FIGHTING TO BELONG!

VOL. I: ASIAN AMERICAN, NATIVE HAWAIIAN, AND PACIFIC ISLANDER HISTORY FROM THE 1700s THROUGH THE 1800s

AMY CHU and ALEXANDER CHANG
Illustrated by LOUIE CHIN

Curriculum Guide by
THE ASIAN AMERICAN EDUCATION PROJECT

THIRD
STATE
BOOKS

LAAUNCH

TAAF

The
Asian
American
Education
Project

San Francisco

FIGHTING TO BELONG!

MEET THE COMMUNITY MIDDLE SCHOOL SEVENTH GRADERS:

SAMMY LEE

AGE: 12

Sammy is into video games, dinosaurs, and soccer. His favorite foods are chicken nuggets, vanilla ice cream, and his grandma's Filipino home cooking. Sammy hates spiders, homework, and anything that might seem boring.

TIANA RODRIGUEZ

AGE: 13

Tiana enjoys honors math, science club, chess club, and Latine club. She reads everything in the library, even historical romance sometimes. Her pet peeves are school bullies and immature classmates.

JOE BYRNE

AGE: 12

Joe likes dogs, anime, and doodling his favorite characters. He plays trumpet in the school band but really wants to switch to drums or bass guitar. On weekends, Joe helps his dad with his construction business, which is why he is a whiz at fixing things.

PADMINI RAO

AGE: 13

Padmini loves dance, cheer squad, and visiting her grandparents in India. Her favorite things to do are karaoke and hanging out with friends. She dislikes insincere people, asparagus, and scary movies. Recently elected Student Council Vice President, Padmini is always there for her friends and fellow students.

KENJI SATO-LOUIS

AGE: 27

Kenji is Tiana's next-door neighbor and works part-time at the American History Museum while he finishes his Ph.D. in American history. Kenji loves teaching and learning new ways to help students, which is why he's also studying illusory thaumaturgic studies (a.k.a. wizardry!) on the side. Kenji is proud of his Haitian and Japanese ancestry. He is named after his grandfather, who was born at the Manzanar incarceration camp in California during World War II.

"CREATE A MULTIMEDIA PROJECT THAT GIVES THE SCHOOL AN OVERVIEW OF AAPI HISTORY."

SO WHAT'S OUR GROUP ASSIGNMENT, PADMINI?

??? WHAT DOES AAPI STAND FOR?

AAPI STANDS FOR "ASIAN AMERICAN AND PACIFIC ISLANDER." IT'S GOING TO BE INTERESTING!

THE ONLY INTERESTING HISTORY IS DINOSAURS. CAN'T WE DO THAT INSTEAD?

THIS CLASS IS ON THE HISTORY OF PEOPLE, SAMMY. DINOSAURS DON'T COUNT.

ACK, YOU'RE KILLING MY DREAMS.

OUR TEXTBOOK HAS HARDLY ANYTHING ON AAPI HISTORY! WHAT ARE WE GOING TO DO? I NEED THIS A...

JOE, HAVE YOU FOUND ANYTHING?

WELL, THERE'S AN EXHIBIT AT THE HISTORY MUSEUM...

REALLY? I THINK MY NEIGHBOR WORKS THERE.

SWEET! TIANA CAN GET US A VIP TOUR!

6

SAMMY: so we really doing this museum trip?

PADMINI: we have to. It's a special exhibit that ends this month

TIANA: My neighbor is one of the tour guides there.

TIANA: He agreed to give us a personal tour, so it's a good opportunity.

JOE: Plus we could get all of the research we need done there.

SAMMY: ok is there a food court

TIANA: SAMMY!

JOE: There is a cafeteria...

SAMMY: 👍

PADMINI: yay! See you all there! let's do our best everyone!

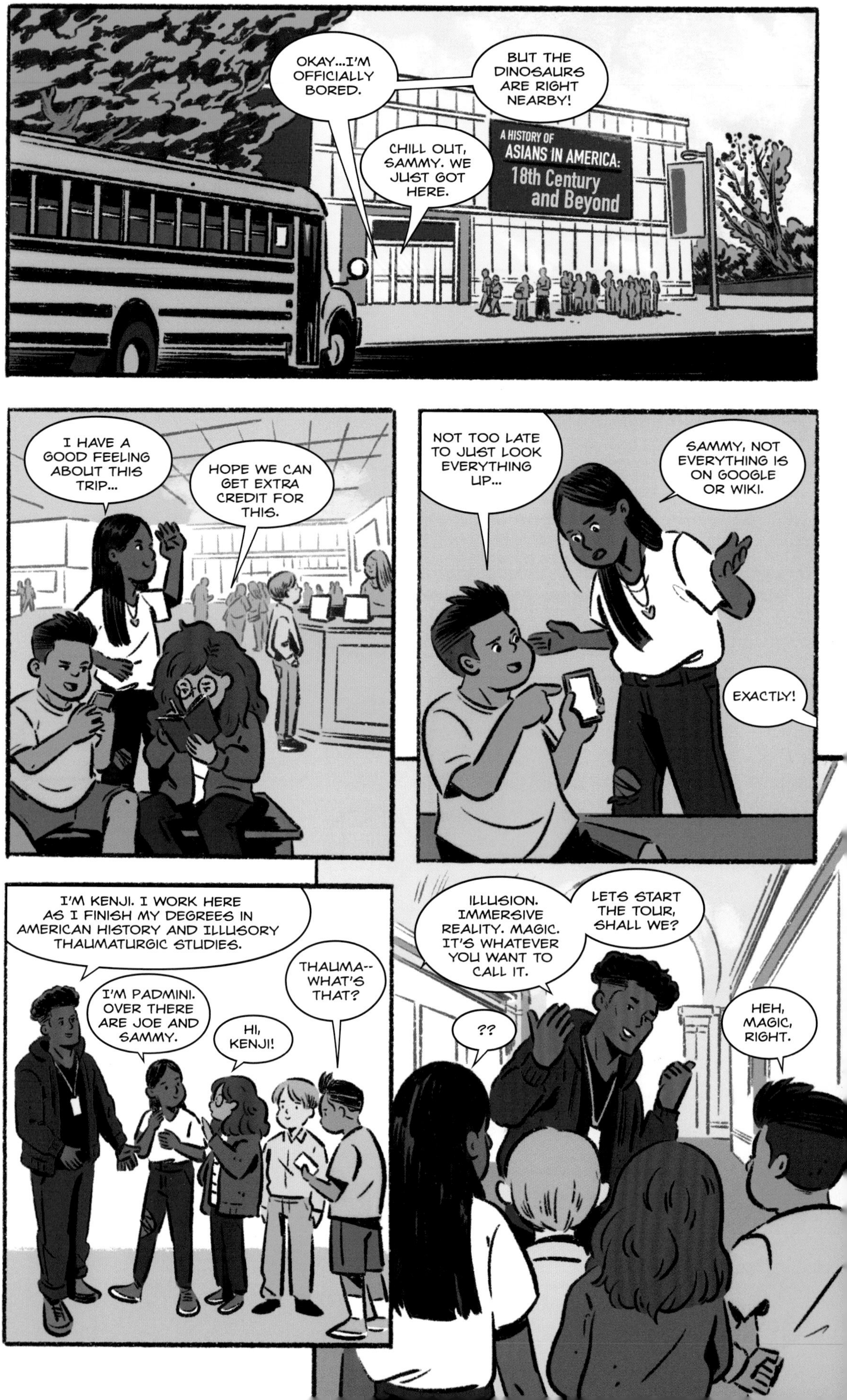
OKAY...I'M OFFICIALLY BORED.
BUT THE DINOSAURS ARE RIGHT NEARBY!
CHILL OUT, SAMMY. WE JUST GOT HERE.
A HISTORY OF ASIANS IN AMERICA: 18th Century and Beyond
I HAVE A GOOD FEELING ABOUT THIS TRIP...
HOPE WE CAN GET EXTRA CREDIT FOR THIS.
NOT TOO LATE TO JUST LOOK EVERYTHING UP...
SAMMY, NOT EVERYTHING IS ON GOOGLE OR WIKI.
EXACTLY!
I'M KENJI. I WORK HERE AS I FINISH MY DEGREES IN AMERICAN HISTORY AND ILLUSORY THAUMATURGIC STUDIES.
I'M PADMINI. OVER THERE ARE JOE AND SAMMY.
HI, KENJI!
THAUMA--WHAT'S THAT?
ILLUSION. IMMERSIVE REALITY. MAGIC. IT'S WHATEVER YOU WANT TO CALL IT.
LETS START THE TOUR, SHALL WE?
??
HEH, MAGIC, RIGHT.

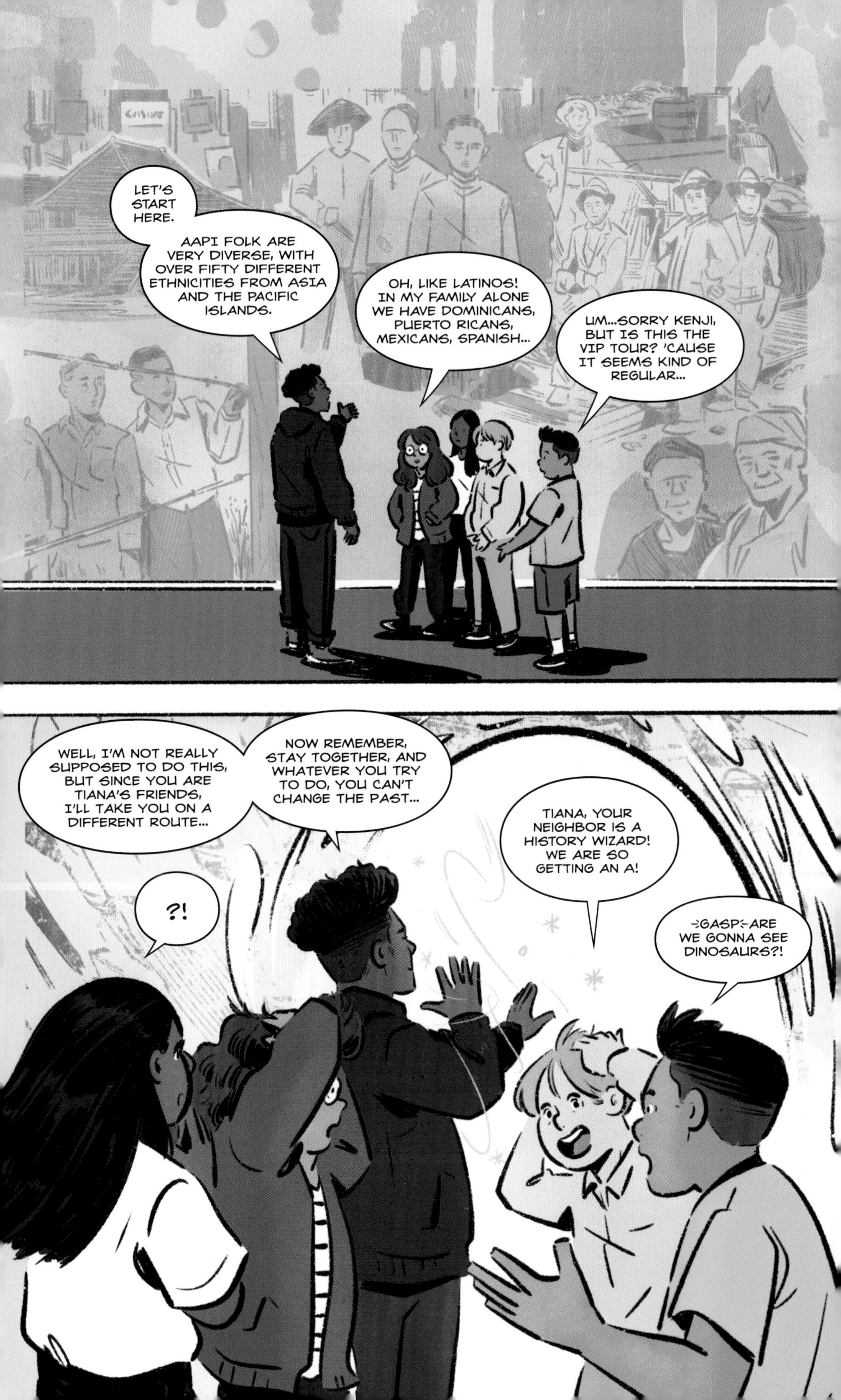
LET'S START HERE.
AAPI FOLK ARE VERY DIVERSE, WITH OVER FIFTY DIFFERENT ETHNICITIES FROM ASIA AND THE PACIFIC ISLANDS.
OH, LIKE LATINOS! IN MY FAMILY ALONE WE HAVE DOMINICANS, PUERTO RICANS, MEXICANS, SPANISH...
UM...SORRY KENJI, BUT IS THIS THE VIP TOUR? 'CAUSE IT SEEMS KIND OF REGULAR...
WELL, I'M NOT REALLY SUPPOSED TO DO THIS, BUT SINCE YOU ARE TIANA'S FRIENDS, I'LL TAKE YOU ON A DIFFERENT ROUTE...
NOW REMEMBER, STAY TOGETHER, AND WHATEVER YOU TRY TO DO, YOU CAN'T CHANGE THE PAST...
?!
TIANA, YOUR NEIGHBOR IS A HISTORY WIZARD! WE ARE SO GETTING AN A!
-GASP- ARE WE GONNA SEE DINOSAURS?!

IS THAT THE OCEAN??

WATCH YOUR STEP, KIDS! WELCOME TO LOUISIANA IN 1763...

THE MANILAMEN

SAMMY, TIANA TELLS ME YOU'RE PART FILIPINO?

WHEN THE SPANISH LANDED HERE OVER 200 YEARS AGO, INDENTURED FILIPINO SAILORS JUMPED SHIP TO ESCAPE...

YEAH, ON MY MOM'S SIDE.

...AND BUILT THIS FISHING VILLAGE.

ST. MALO, LOUISIANA

ARE THOSE STILTS?!

YES, JUST LIKE THEIR HOUSES IN THE PHILIPPINES!

"ALMOST FIFTY YEARS LATER, SONS AND GRANDSONS OF THE MANILAMEN JOINED THE PIRATE JEAN LAFITTE TO HELP DEFEAT THE BRITISH IN THE WAR OF 1812 AND THE BATTLE OF NEW ORLEANS."

FILIPINO CULTURE IS A PART OF LOUISIANA FOOD AND TRADITIONS. THE SHRIMP DANCE IS STILL USED TODAY TO DESHELL THE DAILY CATCH.

OOH, THIS LOOKS FUN!

THIS MARKER COMMEMORATES THEIR EXISTENCE AS THE OLDEST AAPI SETTLER COMMUNITY IN AMERICA.

I HAD NO IDEA! MY PEOPLE!!

EW! SHRIMP SHELLS!

MANILA VILLAGE

KENJI, HOW DO YOU KNOW SO MUCH ABOUT AAPI HISTORY?

WELL, IT'S MY HERITAGE, TOO.

MY MOM'S HAITIAN, BUT MY DAD'S A FOURTH-GENERATION JAPANESE AMERICAN FROM HAWAII. HE NAMED ME KENJI AFTER HIS GRANDFATHER.

OKAY, SO? I'M ALSO PART CHINESE. JOE HERE IS IRISH AND GERMAN. I WANT TO SEE MORE MAGIC!

CAN WE GO, LIKE, TO THE JURASSIC PERIOD?!

SAMMY, HE'S NOT YOUR PERSONAL TIME LORD. I APOLOGIZE ON BEHALF OF MY CLASSMATE.

NO WORRIES. I'M HAPPY TO PRACTICE MY TIME-TRAVEL SKILLS!

I'M NOT GOING TO TAKE YOU TO THE JURASSIC PERIOD, BUT HOW ABOUT THE 19TH CENTURY, WHEN THE FIRST CHINESE ARRIVED?

IN 1820, THERE WERE ONLY A FEW HUNDRED LIVING IN CALIFORNIA. BUT THEN, IN 1849, SOMETHING HAPPENED...

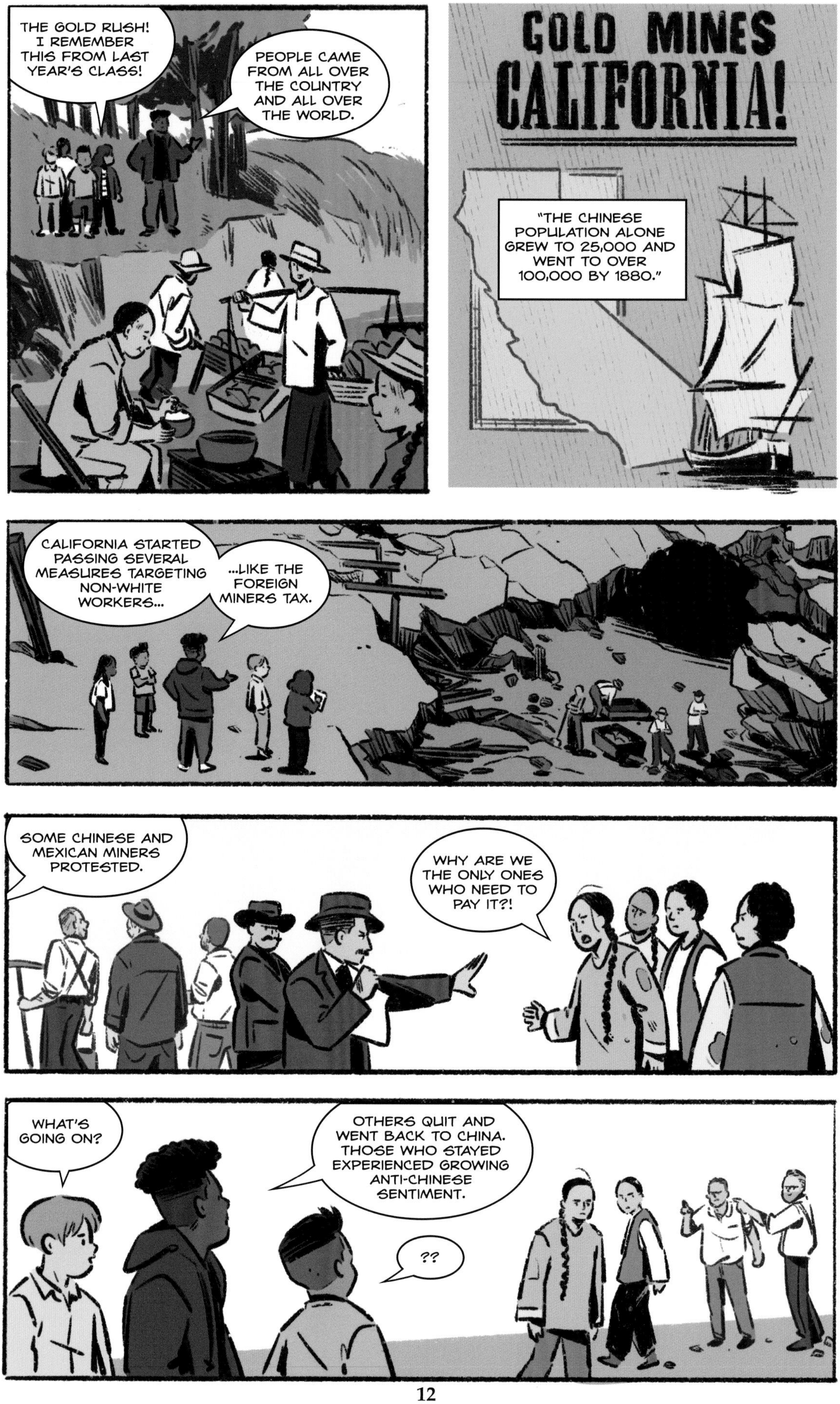
THE GOLD RUSH! I REMEMBER THIS FROM LAST YEAR'S CLASS!
PEOPLE CAME FROM ALL OVER THE COUNTRY AND ALL OVER THE WORLD.
GOLD MINES CALIFORNIA!
"THE CHINESE POPULATION ALONE GREW TO 25,000 AND WENT TO OVER 100,000 BY 1880."
CALIFORNIA STARTED PASSING SEVERAL MEASURES TARGETING NON-WHITE WORKERS...
...LIKE THE FOREIGN MINERS TAX.
SOME CHINESE AND MEXICAN MINERS PROTESTED.
WHY ARE WE THE ONLY ONES WHO NEED TO PAY IT?!
WHAT'S GOING ON?
OTHERS QUIT AND WENT BACK TO CHINA. THOSE WHO STAYED EXPERIENCED GROWING ANTI-CHINESE SENTIMENT.
??

CHINAMEN GETTIN' TO BE ALTOGETHER TOO PLENTIFUL HERE...

"ANTI-CHINESE VIOLENCE CONTINUED TO INCREASE."

"200 CHINESE MINERS WERE ROBBED AND FOUR MURDERED AT RICH GULCH IN MAY 1852."

SAMMY, WHAT ARE YOU DOING?!

STOP MESSING AROUND!

BUT I CAN HELP! THAT'S SO UNFAIR!

"A MINER NAMED LING SING WAS MURDERED. GEORGE HALL AND TWO OTHER MEN WERE ARRESTED."

PEOPLE V. HALL, 1854

THE CALIFORNIA SUPREME COURT RULED THAT BLACK, NATIVE AMERICAN, MIXED-RACE, AND CHINESE PEOPLE COULDN'T TESTIFY AGAINST PEOPLE OF EUROPEAN DESCENT.

GEORGE HALL WAS SET FREE.

SO HE GOT AWAY WITH MURDER, IS WHAT YOU'RE SAYING...

I DON'T KNOW THAT I LIKE THIS STORY AT ALL. WHY DO WE HAVE TO COVER ALL THIS, KENJI?!

HISTORY IS ABOUT TRUTH. WE CAN'T PICK AND CHOOSE ONLY THE NICE PARTS.

SAMMY, IT'S JUST A SCHOOL PROJECT.

NO, NOT ANYMORE. IT'S REAL HISTORY AND I'M NOT SURE I WANT THIS TRUTH STUFF.

MAYBE THIS WAS A MISTAKE. I DON'T WANT TO GET IN TROUBLE WITH YOUR PARENTS. DO YOU WANT TO GO BACK?

NAH, IT'S COOL. LET'S KEEP GOING.

FOR MANY CHINESE THE GOLD RUSH WAS OVER BY THE TIME THEY ARRIVED. SO THEY TURNED TO OTHER JOBS...

MAKES SENSE. LIKE WHAT?

ISN'T THIS WHEN THE TRANSCONTINENTAL RAILROAD WAS BEING BUILT?

THAT'S RIGHT, TIANA! WITH AMERICA EXPANDING WESTWARD, THE COUNTRY WANTED TO FIND A FASTER AND BETTER WAY TO TRAVEL.

OH WOW!

I KNEW IT!

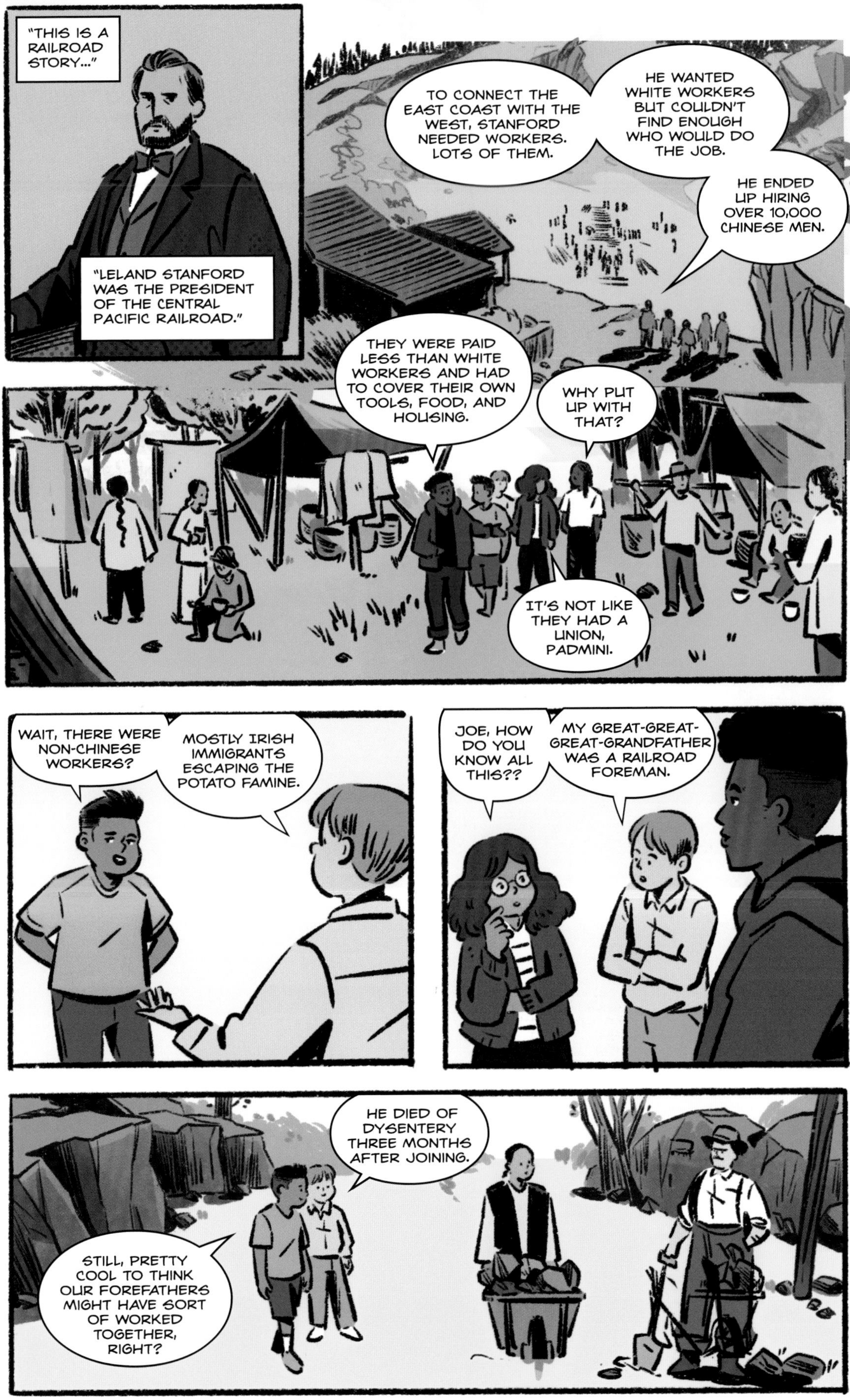
"THIS IS A RAILROAD STORY..."
"LELAND STANFORD WAS THE PRESIDENT OF THE CENTRAL PACIFIC RAILROAD."
TO CONNECT THE EAST COAST WITH THE WEST, STANFORD NEEDED WORKERS. LOTS OF THEM.
HE WANTED WHITE WORKERS BUT COULDN'T FIND ENOUGH WHO WOULD DO THE JOB.
HE ENDED UP HIRING OVER 10,000 CHINESE MEN.
THEY WERE PAID LESS THAN WHITE WORKERS AND HAD TO COVER THEIR OWN TOOLS, FOOD, AND HOUSING.
WHY PUT UP WITH THAT?
IT'S NOT LIKE THEY HAD A UNION, PADMINI.
WAIT, THERE WERE NON-CHINESE WORKERS?
MOSTLY IRISH IMMIGRANTS ESCAPING THE POTATO FAMINE.
JOE, HOW DO YOU KNOW ALL THIS??
MY GREAT-GREAT-GREAT-GRANDFATHER WAS A RAILROAD FOREMAN.
HE DIED OF DYSENTERY THREE MONTHS AFTER JOINING.
STILL, PRETTY COOL TO THINK OUR FOREFATHERS MIGHT HAVE SORT OF WORKED TOGETHER, RIGHT?

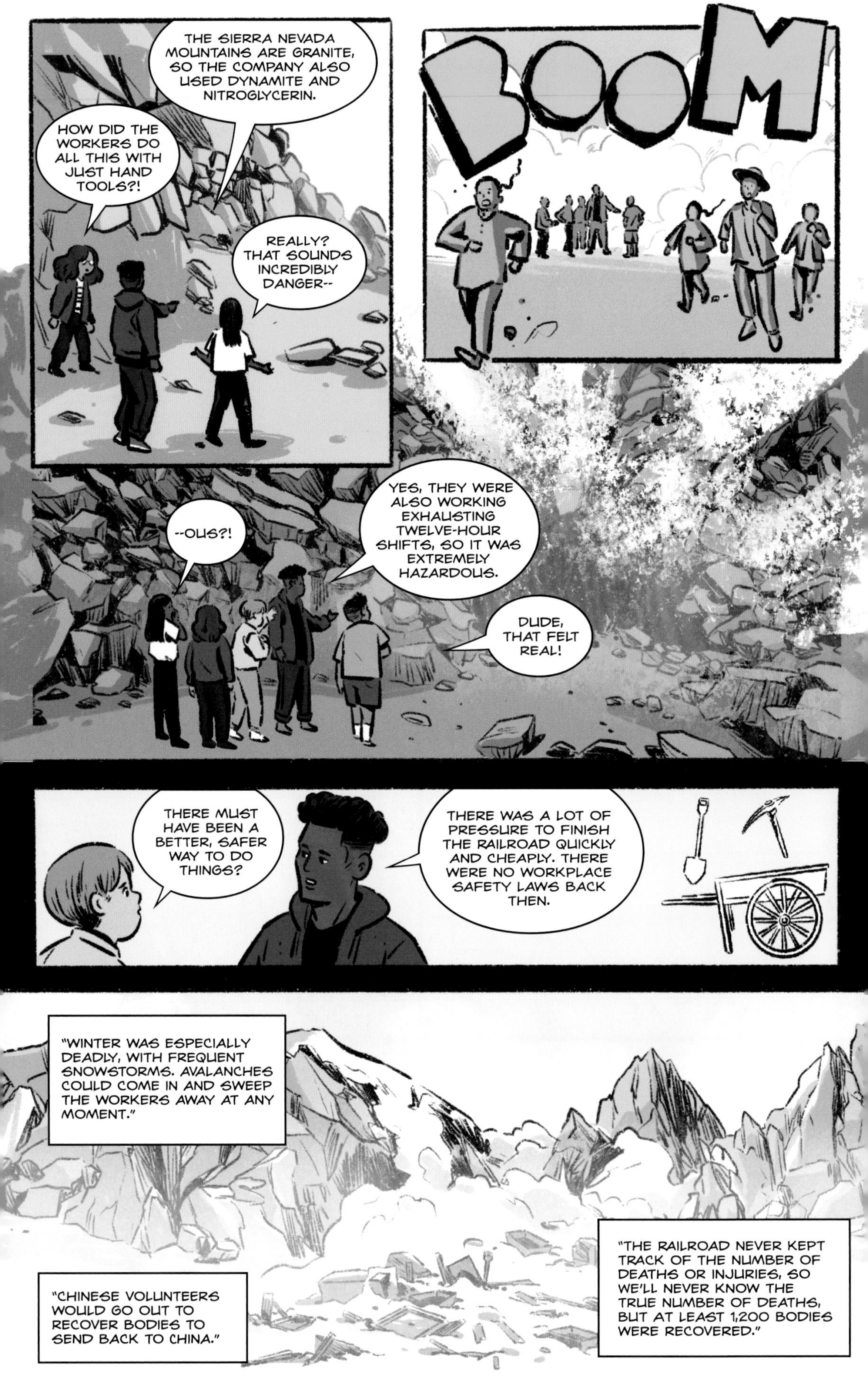
HOW DID THE WORKERS DO ALL THIS WITH JUST HAND TOOLS?!
THE SIERRA NEVADA MOUNTAINS ARE GRANITE, SO THE COMPANY ALSO USED DYNAMITE AND NITROGLYCERIN.
REALLY? THAT SOUNDS INCREDIBLY DANGER--
BOOM
--OUS?!
YES, THEY WERE ALSO WORKING EXHAUSTING TWELVE-HOUR SHIFTS, SO IT WAS EXTREMELY HAZARDOUS.
DUDE, THAT FELT REAL!
THERE MUST HAVE BEEN A BETTER, SAFER WAY TO DO THINGS?
THERE WAS A LOT OF PRESSURE TO FINISH THE RAILROAD QUICKLY AND CHEAPLY. THERE WERE NO WORKPLACE SAFETY LAWS BACK THEN.
"WINTER WAS ESPECIALLY DEADLY, WITH FREQUENT SNOWSTORMS. AVALANCHES COULD COME IN AND SWEEP THE WORKERS AWAY AT ANY MOMENT."
"CHINESE VOLUNTEERS WOULD GO OUT TO RECOVER BODIES TO SEND BACK TO CHINA."
"THE RAILROAD NEVER KEPT TRACK OF THE NUMBER OF DEATHS OR INJURIES, SO WE'LL NEVER KNOW THE TRUE NUMBER OF DEATHS, BUT AT LEAST 1,200 BODIES WERE RECOVERED."

"BECAUSE OF THE HARSH CONDITIONS AND UNEQUAL PAY, THE CHINESE WORKERS STAGED A STRIKE IN 1867, THE LARGEST ORGANIZED LABOR MOVEMENT AT THAT TIME."

"THE COMPANY BROKE THE STRIKE BY CUTTING OFF FOOD AND SUPPLIES AND BRINGING IN ARMED MEN."

"AFTER SIX YEARS, THE TRANSCONTINENTAL RAILROAD WAS COMPLETED. STANFORD HIMSELF CONNECTED THE TWO TRACKS WITH A GOLDEN SPIKE IN A 'LAST SPIKE' CEREMONY. A GROUP PHOTO WAS ARRANGED WITH THE CHIEF ENGINEERS, POLITICIANS, SOLDIERS, AND WHITE RAILROAD WORKERS."

"NONE OF THE CHINESE WERE INCLUDED."

"IN 2014, CORKY LEE, AN ACTIVIST AND PHOTOGRAPHER, CORRECTED THIS BY TAKING A NEW PHOTO WITH DESCENDANTS OF THE CHINESE WORKERS."

SO... I GUESS OUR ANCESTORS MADE HISTORY BUILDING THE RAILROAD?

YES! IT MEANT CROSS-COUNTRY TRAVEL AND TRANSPORTATION ONLY TOOK DAYS INSTEAD OF MONTHS.

KENJI, WHAT HAPPENED TO ALL THE WORKERS? WHERE DID THEY GO?

WELL, SOME RETURNED TO CHINA. THOSE WHO STAYED WERE UNWELCOME IN MANY TOWNS...

SO THEY FORMED THEIR OWN COMMUNITIES.

YOU MEAN CHINATOWNS! I LOVE EATING AND SHOPPING THERE!

IT'S NOT ALL ABOUT SHOPPING AND EATING, PADMINI. LIKE, PEOPLE LIVE THERE, TOO.

ACTUALLY, I WOULDN'T MIND A SNACK...

HEY, I'M NOT SEEING A LOT OF KIDS AND FAMILIES. WHY IS THAT?

GOOD QUESTION! IT WASN'T BY CHOICE. SOME WORKERS HAD WIVES AND KIDS IN CHINA...

BUT THEY WEREN'T ALLOWED TO BRING THEM TO THE U.S. PEOPLE DIDN'T WANT THE CHINESE TO SETTLE DOWN.

WHAT'S GOING ON?

UM, I HAVE A BAD FEELING ABOUT THIS...

IT SOUNDS LIKE SOMEONE'S IN TROUBLE...?

WHAT SHOULD WE DO, PADMINI?!

~GASP~ WHY ARE THEY FIGHTING EACH OTHER?

LOS ANGELES CHINESE MASSACRE OF 1871

"CHINATOWNS WERE GENERALLY PEACEFUL, BUT SOME RESIDENTS ALSO ENGAGED IN CRIMINAL ACTIVITY. THERE WERE DISPUTES AND RIVALRIES. DURING ONE SUCH FIGHT, THE CROSSFIRE WOUNDED A POLICE OFFICER AND KILLED A LOCAL WHITE RANCHER."

"WORD SPREAD AND A MOB OF FIVE HUNDRED PEOPLE GATHERED FOR REVENGE AGAINST THE CHINESE."

THEY LOOTED CHINESE STORES AND ATTACKED INNOCENT BYSTANDERS.

GET OUTTA OUR COUNTRY. YOU PEOPLE DON'T BELONG HERE!!

HEY, LEAVE THEM ALONE!

STOP, SAMMY! REMEMBER WHAT KENJI SAID?! WE CAN'T CHANGE THE PAST!

"IN THE END, NINETEEN MEN AND BOYS WERE SHOT AND LYNCHED."

SORRY I GOT WORKED UP. I DON'T KNOW WHY. I FEEL KINDA SILLY.

IT'S NOT SILLY. I GOT UPSET, TOO. IT'S NOT JUST A SCHOOL PROJECT ANYMORE.

SAMMY, IT'S NOT TOO LATE TO GO BACK...

NO. I DIDN'T THINK I WANTED TO LEARN ABOUT ALL THIS STUFF, BUT I ACTUALLY DO.

IT'S JUST THAT DINOSAURS WERE A LOT SIMPLER TO UNDERSTAND.

THIS IS ALL MY FAULT! I SHOULD HAVE STUCK TO THE REGULAR TOUR.

NO. I WANT TO KNOW MORE. WE CAN KEEP GOING.

"OKAY. WHAT JUST HAPPENED WAS THE CHINESE MASSACRE OF 1871, ONE OF THE LARGEST MASS LYNCHINGS IN U.S. HISTORY."

"MANY OF THE PEOPLE KILLED WERE LEFT WITHOUT A PROPER BURIAL OR OBITUARIES, SO WE DON'T EVEN KNOW THEIR NAMES."

"IN 1885, IN ROCK SPRINGS, WYOMING, 28 CHINESE WERE KILLED, 15 WOUNDED, AND ALL OF THEIR HOMES WERE LOOTED AND BURNED."

KENJI, TELL ME PEOPLE WENT TO JAIL, RIGHT?!

SORRY, NO. ANTI-CHINESE SENTIMENT CONTINUED TO INCREASE ACROSS THE COUNTRY...

IT WASN'T JUST CHINESE. MY PARENTS TOLD ME ABOUT A RACE RIOT AGAINST SOUTH ASIANS IN WASHINGTON IN THE EARLY 1900S...

YOU'RE RIGHT, PADMINI. ANTI-ASIAN SENTIMENT GREW WITH THE ARRIVAL OF IMMIGRANTS FROM DIFFERENT ASIAN COUNTRIES.

YOUR PARENTS WERE TALKING ABOUT THE BELLINGHAM RACE RIOTS OF 1907. A MOB ATTACKED SOUTH ASIAN WORKERS TO PREVENT THEM FROM WORKING IN THE LUMBER MILLS.

WE'LL COVER THAT FOR SURE. RIGHT NOW, LET'S TALK ABOUT THE FIRST ANTI-ASIAN LAW, THE PAGE ACT.

PAGE ACT of 1875

WHAT'S THE PAGE ACT?

BASICALLY, THE PURPOSE WAS TO STOP CHINESE FROM SETTLING DOWN IN THE U.S. BY RESTRICTING WOMEN FROM ENTERING.

"IT WAS FOLLOWED BY THE CHINESE EXCLUSION ACT SEVEN YEARS LATER, WHICH BARRED MOST CHINESE FROM IMMIGRATING TO AMERICA."

THIS WAS THE FIRST AMERICAN ACT THAT EXCLUDED IMMIGRANTS BASED ON RACE. THEN, SOMETHING UNEXPECTED HAPPENED IN 1906...

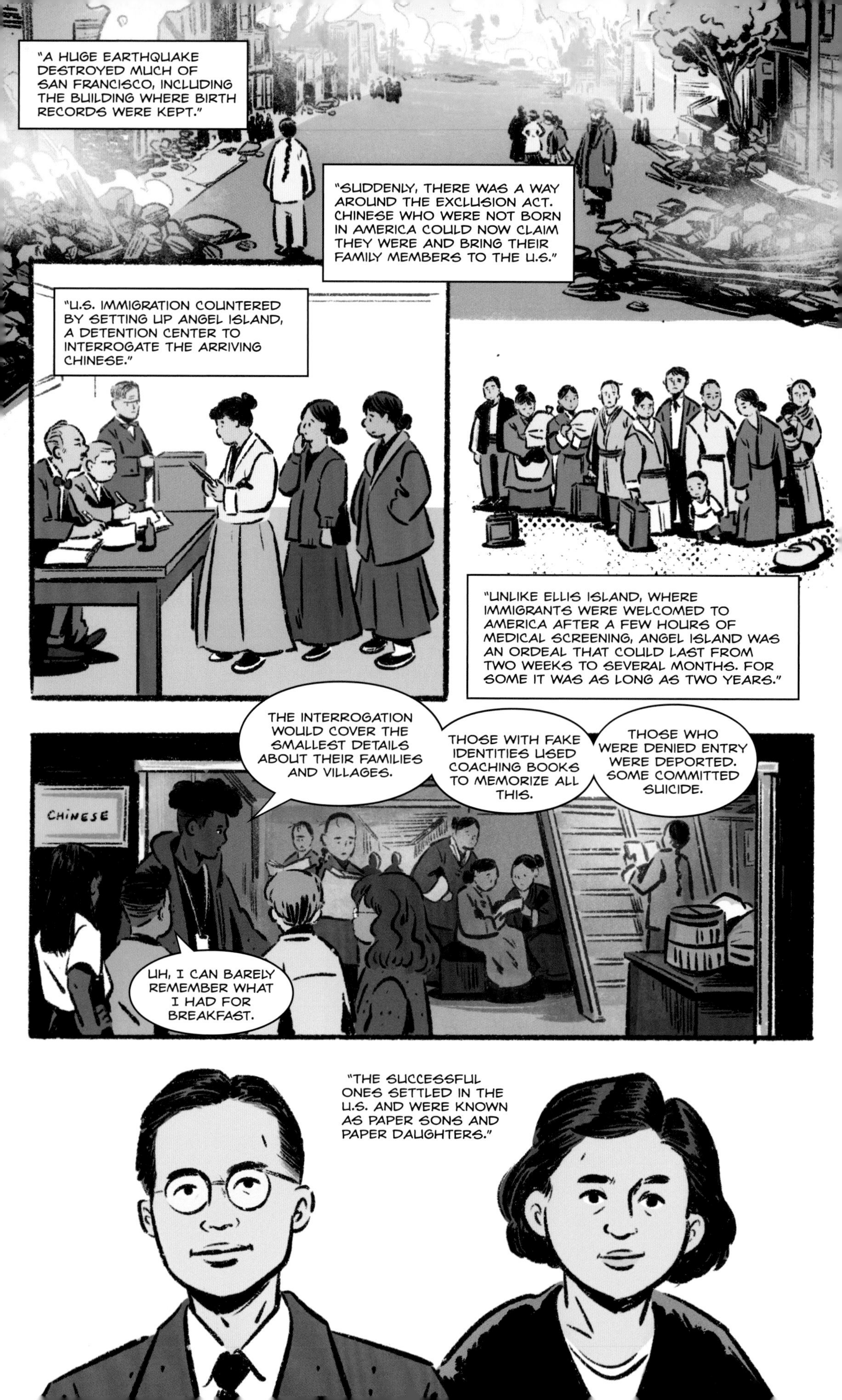

"A HUGE EARTHQUAKE DESTROYED MUCH OF SAN FRANCISCO, INCLUDING THE BUILDING WHERE BIRTH RECORDS WERE KEPT."
"SUDDENLY, THERE WAS A WAY AROUND THE EXCLUSION ACT. CHINESE WHO WERE NOT BORN IN AMERICA COULD NOW CLAIM THEY WERE AND BRING THEIR FAMILY MEMBERS TO THE U.S."
"U.S. IMMIGRATION COUNTERED BY SETTING UP ANGEL ISLAND, A DETENTION CENTER TO INTERROGATE THE ARRIVING CHINESE."
"UNLIKE ELLIS ISLAND, WHERE IMMIGRANTS WERE WELCOMED TO AMERICA AFTER A FEW HOURS OF MEDICAL SCREENING, ANGEL ISLAND WAS AN ORDEAL THAT COULD LAST FROM TWO WEEKS TO SEVERAL MONTHS. FOR SOME IT WAS AS LONG AS TWO YEARS."
CHINESE
THE INTERROGATION WOULD COVER THE SMALLEST DETAILS ABOUT THEIR FAMILIES AND VILLAGES.
THOSE WITH FAKE IDENTITIES USED COACHING BOOKS TO MEMORIZE ALL THIS.
THOSE WHO WERE DENIED ENTRY WERE DEPORTED. SOME COMMITTED SUICIDE.
UH, I CAN BARELY REMEMBER WHAT I HAD FOR BREAKFAST.
"THE SUCCESSFUL ONES SETTLED IN THE U.S. AND WERE KNOWN AS PAPER SONS AND PAPER DAUGHTERS."

SO THESE PAPER SONS AND DAUGHTERS HAD FAMILIES?

FAMILIES WERE IN THE MINORITY AT FIRST. CHINATOWNS STARTED OFF AS BACHELOR SOCIETIES.

CHINESE AND OTHER ASIANS WERE NOT ALLOWED TO OWN PROPERTY OUTSIDE CHINATOWN OR EVEN ATTEND PUBLIC SCHOOLS.

ISN'T THAT ILLEGAL, KENJI?

WELL, NOT AT FIRST. WE HAD TO FIGHT FOR THOSE RIGHTS.

SPRING VALLEY SCHOOL, SAN FRANCISCO, CA, 1884

AND WE SHOULD THANK ONE FAMILY IN PARTICULAR WHO PERSISTED IN CHALLENGING THE STATUS QUO.

"JOSEPH AND MARY TAPE WERE BORN IN CHINA BUT GREW UP IN THE U.S. JOSEPH WAS A SUCCESSFUL BUSINESSMAN AND MARY WAS A TALENTED PHOTOGRAPHER AND PIANIST. THEY GOT MARRIED AND HAD THEIR FIRST CHILD A YEAR LATER."

"WHEN IT WAS TIME, MAMIE TRIED TO ENROLL IN THE LOCAL SCHOOL BUT WAS TURNED AWAY FOR BEING CHINESE."

"MAMIE'S PARENTS SUED THE PRINCIPAL AND THE SAN FRANCISCO BOARD OF EDUCATION. THE CASE WENT TO THE CALIFORNIA SUPREME COURT."

"THE COURT RULED IN FAVOR OF THE TAPE FAMILY, SAYING THAT PUBLIC EDUCATION HAD TO BE OPEN TO ALL CHILDREN."

RIGHT ON! SO THEY WON!

YES AND NO. THE SCHOOL INSISTED THERE WAS NO ROOM FOR MAMIE.

THEY SET UP A SEPARATE SCHOOL FOR HER AND THE OTHER CHINESE KIDS.

WHAT? THAT'S SO RIDICULOUS!

"BUT THEIR FIGHT WASN'T FOR NOTHING. MANY YEARS LATER, THE SUPREME COURT RULED UNANIMOUSLY THAT RACIAL SEGREGATION OF CHILDREN IN PUBLIC SCHOOLS WAS UNCONSTITUTIONAL, CITING MAMIE'S CASE."

WAIT, YOU'RE TALKING ABOUT THE LANDMARK CIVIL RIGHTS CASE "BROWN VS. THE BOARD OF EDUCATION!"

THAT'S RIGHT, TIANA! LET'S HEAD INTO THE CITY NOW TO LEARN ABOUT ANOTHER IMPORTANT LAWSUIT...

YICK WO V. HOPKINS

IN 1886, MOST LAUNDRIES WERE RUN BY CHINESE. IT WAS ONE OF THE FEW JOBS THEY COULD GET.

SAN FRANCISCO DECIDED TO MAKE IT ILLEGAL TO RUN A LAUNDRY IN A WOODEN BUILDING WITHOUT A PERMIT.

SO EVERYONE GOT A PERMIT?

THEY DID GIVE OUT PERMITS, BUT PRETTY MUCH TO ONLY THE NON-CHINESE OWNERS.

OH. I SEE.

YICK WO RAN HIS LAUNDRY ANYWAY AND WAS ARRESTED BY SHERIFF PETER HOPKINS.

THAT SEEMS... WRONG.

THE CHINESE LAUNDRY OWNERS THOUGHT SO, TOO. THEY SUED.

THE JUDGE RULED THAT THE CHINESE WERE PROTECTED UNDER THE 14TH AMENDMENT.

THE 14TH AMENDMENT USED TO ABOLISH SLAVERY?

"YES. HE SAID THE LAW ITSELF WAS NOT DISCRIMINATORY BUT WAS USED TO DISCRIMINATE AGAINST THE CHINESE."

BY THE 1950S, THE YICK WO RULING WAS USED TO STOP SEVERAL ATTEMPTS TO LIMIT THE RIGHTS OF OTHER MINORITIES.

SO HE WON! AWESOME!

WOULD THAT BE HAWAI'I?!

SWEET!

LET'S HEAD TO A STATE WHERE ASIANS AND PACIFIC ISLANDERS ARE THE MAJORITY OF THE POPULATION...

YOU KEEP SAYING "PACIFIC ISLANDERS," BUT WHO DOES THAT INCLUDE?

WELL, HAWAIIANS AND SAMOANS FOR SURE.

HEY, IT'S GETTING WARMER!

YES, TIANA, BUT ALSO PEOPLE FROM GUAM, FIJI, TONGA...

"ALSO CHAMORU AND MARSHALLESE PEOPLE...

AND ANYONE FROM MELANESIA, MICRONESIA, AND POLYNESIA.

MICRONESIA

POLYNESIA

MELANESIA

THERE ARE OVER A MILLION PACIFIC ISLANDERS THROUGHOUT THE UNITED STATES, WITH OVER A THIRD LIVING IN HAWAI'I.

ASIANS CAME TO HAWAI'I LARGELY BECAUSE OF THE SUGAR PLANTATIONS STARTED BY U.S. BUSINESSMEN IN THE LATE 19TH CENTURY."

THE PLANTATIONS RECRUITED FROM CHINA, JAPAN, KOREA, AND THE PHILIPPINES.

PAY WAS LOW AND WORK CONDITIONS WERE HARSH. MANY WORKERS WENT BACK, BUT SOME STAYED.

WHAT ABOUT THE NATIVE HAWAIIANS?

KINGDOM OF HAWAI'I, 1885

"THE NATIVE HAWAIIANS WEREN'T HAPPY WITH THE PLANTATIONS. THEIR LAND WAS TAKEN, THEIR LABOR EXPLOITED, AND THE POPULATION WAS DECIMATED BY DISEASES BROUGHT BY FOREIGNERS."

"CHIEF KAMEHAMEHA I MAY HAVE BEEN SUCCESSFUL IN UNITING THE HAWAIIAN ISLANDS UNDER THE KINGDOM OF HAWAI'I IN 1810. BUT HE WAS NOT ABLE TO PREVENT THE OUTCOME OF WHAT FOREIGNERS BROUGHT TO THE ISLANDS. HIS OWN SON DIED OF MEASLES CONTRACTED FROM THE BRITISH."

"LILI'UOKALANI WAS A MUSICIAN AND TALENTED COMPOSER. WHEN SHE BECAME QUEEN IN 1891, SHE WANTED HAWAI'I TO RETAIN ITS INDEPENDENCE."

"SHE WAS OVERTHROWN BY A GROUP OF AMERICAN SUGAR PLANTATION OWNERS AND BUSINESSMEN WITH THE HELP OF U.S. TROOPS."

"HAWAI'I BECAME AN AMERICAN TERRITORY IN 1898..."

"AND IN 1959, IT BECAME THE 50TH U.S. STATE, DESPITE THE PROTESTS OF MANY NATIVE HAWAIIANS."

"THE SUGAR INDUSTRY HAD ALWAYS RELIED ON INEXPENSIVE LABOR. AS WORKERS BECAME MORE AND MORE EFFECTIVE IN ORGANIZING LABOR STRIKES, STATEHOOD ENDED UP GIVING THEM EVEN MORE RIGHTS AS U.S. CITIZENS. THE COMPANIES BEGAN SHIFTING PRODUCTION TO OTHER CHEAPER COUNTRIES, LIKE CUBA."

"ON NOVEMBER 23, 1993, CONGRESS PASSED PUBLIC LAW 103-150, FINALLY ACKNOWLEDGING AND APOLOGIZING FOR THE AMERICAN ROLE IN OVERTHROWING THE HAWAIIAN MONARCHY."

"TODAY, THERE ARE NO MORE SUGAR PLANTATIONS LEFT IN HAWAI'I, BUT THE NATIVE HAWAIIAN FIGHT FOR SOVEREIGNTY CONTINUES."

THAT WAS AN AMAZING TRIP! I CAN'T BELIEVE WE WENT TO HAWAII!

RIGHT?! I'M AMAZED KENJI TOOK US TO SO MANY PLACES!

YOU CAN ALL THANK ME FOR ASKING ABOUT THE VIP TOUR...

WE'RE GOING TO HAVE THE BEST HISTORY PRESENTATION IN THE WHOLE SCHOOL!

WELL, WE ONLY JUST STARTED THE 20TH CENTURY, SO THERE'S STILL A LOT AHEAD...

SO WHAT'S NEXT?!

THERE YOU ARE!

JAPANESE AMERICANS AND WWII, SOUTHEAST ASIANS POST-VIETNAM WAR, SOUTH ASIANS AND 9/11...

WHERE HAVE YOU BEEN?! YOU'VE BEEN MISSING FOR THE LAST TWO HOURS!

UH, KIDS, THIS IS DR. WERNER, DIRECTOR OF THE MUSEUM.

YOUR BADGE PLEASE, KENJI. YOU'RE FIRED.

BUT...

TO BE CONTINUED...

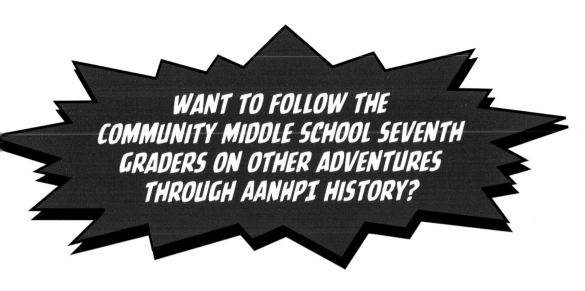

WANT TO FOLLOW THE COMMUNITY MIDDLE SCHOOL SEVENTH GRADERS ON OTHER ADVENTURES THROUGH AANHPI HISTORY?

Check out other books in the
History of Asian Americans, Native Hawaiians,
and Pacific Islanders series!

Volume II (September 2024)

and

Volume III (January 2025)

FIGHTING TO BELONG!
CURRICULUM GUIDE

The information and activities presented here are meant to be used along-side *Fighting to Belong!* and correspond to specific pages and/or topics discussed in the book. The activities aim to build upon and deepen student knowledge. You may choose to implement one or more of the activities and/or teach the relevant lesson(s) on the topic. A full curriculum guide featuring many more lessons and resources is available on The Asian American Education Project's website, asianamericanedu.org. This curriculum guide will be updated regularly with more educational materials being created to support this graphic series. Please stay connected with The Asian American Education Project!

What is AANHPI?

AANHPI is an acronym for Asian American, Native Hawaiian, and Pacific Islander. The AANHPI community generally refers to people with Asian, Native Hawaiian, and/or Pacific Islander ancestry, and AANHPI is one of several names used to identify this group. (AAPI, or Asian American and Pacific Islander, is another widely used acronym.) As descriptors, these names are used to identify people's culture, race, heritage, etc. People can choose to identify as Asian American as well as more specifically, such as Hmong American, Korean American, etc. It's up to the individual.

In addition, these names can be used as a political strategy, serving to unify distinct groups to fight for common goals such as justice and civil rights. As a community, AANHPIs can find strength in numbers, which gives this group more leverage and political power.

Activities:

- Have students research the historical and cultural significance of the terms AAPI, AA&PI, APIDA, and AANHPI. Facilitate a discussion by asking: What is the purpose of each identifier? What are the pros and cons of each term? How are they inclusive? How are they exclusive?

- Have students read the *Time* magazine article entitled "In 1968, These Activists Coined the Term 'Asian American' – and Helped Shape Decades of Advocacy" by Anna Purna Kambhampaty (May 22, 2020). Have them discuss the origins of the Asian American Political Alliance (AAPA), a student group believed to be the first to publicly use the phrase "Asian American."

- Have students research what an "umbrella term" means. Have them explain why and how AAPI is an umbrella term. Have them explain how and why AAPI as an umbrella term can be helpful or problematic.

- Have students look up Asian and/or Pacific Islander countries or regions on a world map. Have them select one country and research how and why people migrated from that region to the United States. Have students create a slide deck summarizing what they learned.

AANHPI History *Is* American History

Background:

History textbooks and school curricula do not sufficiently include AANHPI experiences. A landmark 2022 report by the organization Leading Asian Americans to Unite for Change, called the LAAUNCH STAATUS (Social Tracking of Asian Americans in the United States) Index, found that most Americans cannot name a single prominent Asian American. This suggests that K–12 students are not learning about AANHPI histories and narratives. Today, there are active movements to remedy this, including mandates to include AANHPI content in schools and the development of AANHPI lessons.

Activities:

- Have students create a bubble map about their prior knowledge of AANHPI history. Encourage them to list people, places, events, and more.

- Have them select three ideas and share where they learned the content. Tally the sources of information and analyze how AANHPI content has been learned by the group.

- Have students share all the important Asian Americans, Native Hawaiians, and Pacific Islanders they can recall. With the students, sort the list of names into categories such as politicians, activists, writers, movie stars, inventors, etc. Facilitate a discussion by asking: What do these data tell us about our knowledge of the AANHPI community?

- Create a class pledge to learn more about AANHPI history. Ask students: Why is it important to learn about AANHPI history? How can we commit to learning more?

We Are Not a Monolith

Background:

The AANHPI community is extremely diverse, comprising hundreds of ethnic groups from across Asia and the Pacific Islands. The community's diversity is seen in many other ways, including religion, language, cultural practices, foods, and much more. It's important to not view all AANHPI folks as the same; the AANHPI community is not a monolith. Individual cultures should be viewed as unique and distinct. That being stated, there is value in sharing a common identity as an AANHPI community in that they do share common experiences of exclusion and oppression in the United States.

Activities:

- Have students write "I am from . . ." poems. Have students share their poems with a partner. Have each pair discuss their respective cultural backgrounds and some of their family traditions. Encourage them to note similarities along with the differences.

- Have students conduct oral history interviews with two or three people from an AANHPI background. Have them generate questions to learn more about their migration stories and about their experiences in the United States. Have them summarize their learning by writing a biography or profile for each of their interviewees.

- Have students compare the AANHPI community to the Latine communities and discuss the shared struggles between the two with regard to the diverse groups represented by each.

The Manilamen

Background:

Early Filipino American settlers in Louisiana made a living in the shrimp business as shrimp was abundant in this area. They used a technique called "dancing the shrimp" to remove dried shells from shrimp meat. First, they caught shrimp using nets and then loaded their haul onto their boats. Next, they boiled the shrimp and spread them out to dry. Once dried, they danced on piles of dried shrimp. The stomping action caused the shells to crumble away, leaving only the meat.

Activities:

- Have students research the specific steps of the Filipino shrimp dance technique. Have them create a step-by-step list and then act out the technique.

- Have students compare the Filipino technique for breaking shrimp shells to that of the Chinese. The Chinese would load dried shrimp into bags and then throw the bags in a circular motion over their shoulders. They would repeatedly beat the shrimp against the ground.

- Have students research other techniques for removing shrimp shells, including modern methods. Have them make and justify an argument for the best technique.

- Have students identify and analyze three other ways in which the Manilamen brought Filipino customs and traditions to Louisiana.

- Have students listen to or read oral histories from Filipino cooks in Louisiana. Replicate this project with your class by asking students to choose a beloved dish from their own family and then interview a family member or friend about the dish. Create a collective class cookbook which includes recipes and the historical significance of each dish.

The Transcontinental Railroad

Background:

Between 1863 and 1869, over 13,000 Chinese laborers helped build the Transcontinental Railroad, which revolutionized travel connecting the eastern and western United States. Chinese workers innovated practices to blast through rock and performed the most dangerous tasks, resulting in many deaths and injuries. Despite their contributions, they were discriminated against and overlooked. Perceived to be foreigners due to their dress, language, and customs, these Chinese workers were paid less than other workers and faced much prejudice.

Activities:

- Have students create an infographic of at least ten significant numbers related to the building of the Transcontinental Railroad. Have them explain the numbers and provide visuals as needed. Ensure they include the contributions and the plight of the Chinese workers.

- Have students research what was needed to build the Transcontinental Railroad, the largest engineering project of the time. Then, have students research the contributions of the Chinese who were valued for their expertise of explosives and more. Tell students that all work was done by hand, using carts, shovels, and picks, but no machinery.

- Have students take a virtual tour of the California State Archives' online exhibit "Making the Grade: California and the Transcontinental Railroad." Have students complete a note catcher. An option is to do a jigsaw by assigning small groups to a specific exhibit to research and share.

- Jigsaw students into three groups to study the impacts of the Transcontinental Railroad on these three groups: American businessmen, Native Americans, and Chinese immigrants. Have students create a slide deck summarizing their findings and present them to the class.

The Pacific Islands

Background:

Pacific Islanders are people whose ancestors were the original peoples of Polynesia, Micronesia, and Melanesia. The Pacific Islands have a unique history of sovereignty and colonization. Because of their strategic location in the Pacific Ocean, these islands are a desirable military location; they are also coveted for their natural resources and as tourist destinations. It is important to note that Pacific Islanders have their own unique cultures and histories.

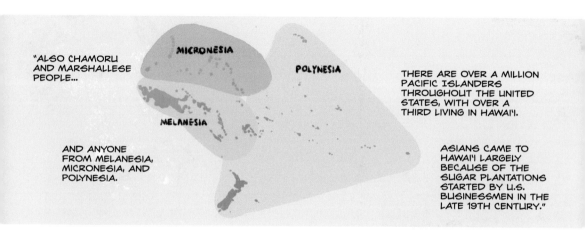

"ALSO CHAMORU AND MARSHALLESE PEOPLE...

MICRONESIA

POLYNESIA

THERE ARE OVER A MILLION PACIFIC ISLANDERS THROUGHOUT THE UNITED STATES, WITH OVER A THIRD LIVING IN HAWAI'I.

MELANESIA

AND ANYONE FROM MELANESIA, MICRONESIA, AND POLYNESIA.

ASIANS CAME TO HAWAI'I LARGELY BECAUSE OF THE SUGAR PLANTATIONS STARTED BY U.S. BUSINESSMEN IN THE LATE 19TH CENTURY."

Activities:

- Have students study a map of the Pacific Islands. Split the class into three groups and assign them to research Polynesia, Micronesia, and Melanesia. Have each group create a slide deck about their assigned areas to share with others. Make sure students include facts about history, languages, cultural traditions, food, etc.

- Have students learn about American exceptionalism and manifest destiny. Facilitate a discussion by asking: How do these concepts relate to the United States' colonization of the Pacific Islands? How did colonization affect the islands?

- Tell students that American Samoa, Guam, and the Northern Mariana Islands are U.S. territories. Have students research what it means to be a territory versus a state.

Hawai'i

Background:

In 1795, Kamehameha I (1758–1819) unified the Hawaiian islands under one kingdom and became its first ruler. (Previously, ancient Hawaiian society consisted of a series of tribes.) The kingdom of Hawai'i was an independent constitutional monarchy modeled after European monarchies.

Increased contact with Europe and America brought merchants, missionaries, and businessmen, who established sugar plantations and recruited Asian workers from China, Japan, Korea, and the Philippines. Native Hawaiians increasingly lost their lands, labor, language, and power. In 1887, the Hawaiian king was forced, at gunpoint, to sign away monarchy powers to Americans, Europeans, and Native Hawaiian elites who were focused on profit; this became known as the "Bayonet Constitution."

In 1891, Queen Lili'uokalani (1838–1917) ascended the throne, the kingdom's first female monarch and last monarch. She was committed to restoring the monarch's power, but was overthrown two years later in a coup organized by American sugar planters and backed by the U.S. military, effectively ending the Hawaiian kingdom. In 1898, Hawai'i was annexed as a U.S. territory, and in 1959, it became the 50th U.S. state.

Statehood was controversial. Some Hawaiian residents wanted to have the same rights as other states, such as electing their own governor. However, many Native Hawaiians wanted sovereignty and rejected statehood, which they saw as American imperialism, militarism, and colonization. Activists are still fighting for sovereignty today.

"LILI'UOKALANI WAS A MUSICIAN AND TALENTED COMPOSER. WHEN SHE BECAME QUEEN IN 1891, SHE WANTED HAWAI'I TO RETAIN ITS INDEPENDENCE."

Activities:

- Have students create a timeline of the history of the kingdom of Hawai'i.

- Have students research the negative impacts of foreign influence on Hawai'i, such as climate change, water shortages, the erasure of language and cultures, the introduction of diseases, etc. Have them identify one of the issues and create a commercial promoting a solution to the problem. Encourage them to research what is already being done.

- Tell students that Hawaiians believe they're stewards of the land and oceans. Facilitate a discussion by asking students: What is the American connection to the land? What evidence supports this? How can Americans adopt this Hawaiian concept of stewardship?

- Have some students research reasons why some Native Hawaiians opposed statehood; and have them create protest posters to support their cause. Have other students research reasons why some Hawaiian residents supported statehood; and have them write speeches to support their cause.

- Have students research a Native Hawaiian activist who supports sovereignty and create a movie trailer or short documentary of their life. Host a film festival for students to showcase their work.

Check out the full curriculum guide on The Asian American Education Project's website to access many more lessons and resources!

AFTERWORD

We began this project with a simple question: Why aren't there more books that introduce Asian American, Native Hawaiian, and Pacific Islander (AANHPI) history to students?

AANHPI history *is* American history. But our unique experiences, challenges, and contributions to this country's development are rarely taught in schools, and Americans have little knowledge about our history or confuse it with Asian history. For many Americans of Asian, Native Hawaiian, and Pacific Islander descent who grew up in the United States, there continues to be a startling lack of opportunity to learn about our own history.

We created the History of Asian Americans, Native Hawaiians, and Pacific Islanders series to share our story with you in a medium more engaging than a traditional textbook. *Fighting to Belong!* is the first of a three-volume series that begins with the arrival of the "Manilamen" to American shores in the eighteenth century and covers the next 150 years of AANHPI history. The next two volumes, due in September 2024 and January 2025, will provide highlights of our rich history from the beginning of the twentieth century to today. Highlights of those volumes include the incarceration of Japanese Americans during World War II; the immigration of Southeast Asian refugees and immigrants in the aftermath of the Vietnam Conflict; the challenges faced by South Asian Americans after the 9/11 tragedy; the contributions of AANHPIs to American society and culture; and much more.

We hope the History of Asian Americans, Native Hawaiians, and Pacific Islanders series will reach a new audience—young and old, AANHPIs and non-AANHPIs—across the country and increase understanding of how our history is truly woven into the fabric of American history. Thank you for reading!

Norman Chen
Co-Founder, LAAUNCH
CEO, TAAF